Our Guests

Our Guests

Our Guests

Our Guests

Our Guests

Our Guests

Our Guests

Our Guests

Our Guests

Our Guests

Our Guests

Our Guests

Our Guests

Our Guests

Our Guests

Our Guests

Our Guests

Our Guests

Our Guests

Our Guests

Our Guests

Our Guests

Our Guests

Our Guests

Our Guests

Our Guests

Our Guests

Our Guests

Our Guests

Our Guests

Our Guests

Our Guests

Our Guests

Our Guests

Our Guests

Our Guests

Our Guests

Our Guests

Our Guests

Our Guests

Our Guests

Our Guests

Our Guests

Our Guests

Our Guests

Our Guests

Our Guests

Our Guests

Our Guests

Our Guests

Our Guests

Our Guests

Our Guests

Our Guests

Our Guests

Our Guests

Our Guests

Our Guests

Our Guests

Our Guests

Our Guests

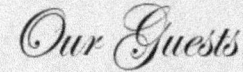

Our Guests

Our Guests

Our Guests

Our Guests

Our Guests

Our Guests

Our Guests

Our Guests

Our Guests

Our Guests

Our Guests

Our Guests

Our Guests

Our Guests

Our Guests

Our Guests

Our Guests

Our Guests

Our Guests

Our Guests

Our Guests

Our Guests

Our Guests

Our Guests

Our Guests

Our Guests

Our Guests

Our Guests

Our Guests

Our Guests

Our Guests

Our Guests

Our Guests

Our Guests

Our Guests

Our Guests

Our Guests

Our Guests

Our Guests

Our Guests

Our Guests

Our Guests

Our Guests

Our Guests

Our Guests

Our Guests

Our Guests

Our Guests

Our Guests

Our Guests

Our Guests

Our Guests

Our Guests

Our Guests

Our Guests

Our Guests

Our Guests

Our Guests

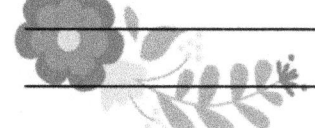

Our Guests

Our Guests

Our Guests

Our Guests

Our Guests

Our Guests

Our Guests

Our Guests

Our Guests

Our Guests

Our Guests

Our Guests

Our Guests

Our Guests

Our Guests

Our Guests

Our Guests

Our Guests

Our Guests

Our Guests

Our Guests

Our Guests

Our Guests

Our Guests

Our Guests

Our Guests

Our Guests

Our Guests

Our Guests

Our Guests

Our Guests

Our Guests

Our Guests

Our Guests

Our Guests

Our Guests

Our Guests

Our Guests

Our Guests

Our Guests

Our Guests

Our Guests

Our Guests

Our Guests

Our Guests

Our Guests

Our Guests

Our Guests

Our Guests

Our Guests

Our Guests

Our Guests

Our Guests

Our Guests

Our Guests

Our Guests

Our Guests

Our Guests

Our Guests

Our Guests

Our Guests

Our Guests

Our Guests

Our Guests

Our Guests

Our Guests

Our Guests

Our Guests

Our Guests

Our Guests

Our Guests

Our Guests

Our Guests

Our Guests

Our Guests

Our Guests

Our Guests

www.ingramcontent.com/pod-product-compliance
Lightning Source LLC
LaVergne TN
LVHW060137080526
838202LV00049B/4015